Lighting Candles 3

Another 31 Day Devotional to Inspire a Closer relationship with God

Terrie Sizemore

This is a work of non-fiction.
Text and illustrations are copyrighted by
Terrie Sizemore, DVM, RN ©2020

Library of Congress Control Number: 2020904735
All rights reserved.

No part of this book may be
reproduced, transmitted, or stored in an
information retrieval
system in any form or by any means,
graphic, electronic, or mechanical without prior
written permission from the author.

First Edition 2020
Printed in the United States of America
A 2 Z Press LLC
PO Box 582
Deleon Springs, FL 32130
bestlittleonlinebookstore.com
sizemore3630@aol.com
440-241-3126
ISBN: 978-1-946908-20-9

Dedication

*This book is dedicated to her father,
Edwin Sizemore.
I thank him for believing for and
praying for me to have faith.*

Day 1- The Ax Floated

I have read the different stories about Elijah and Elisha for years. Great stories! Great men of God. Some of my favorites include Elijah blessing a widow woman and her son so they never ran out of food even when she thought she was making her last meal. (1 Kings 17.16)

Another favorite is when the Word of God came to Elijah for the same widow woman to have a son, that son died, and Elijah prayed for him to live again! (1 Kings 17) He prays for rain (1 Kings 18), was protected by God (2 Kings 1), parted waters with his mantle being placed on the ground (2 Kings 2.8), and conferred his anointing to Elisha who asked for a double portion of Elijah's anointing! (2 Kings 2.9-15)!

Elisha continued to walk in the same great anointing as Elijah - especially when he cast salt in spring water to heal that water that was causing death, miscarriage, and barrenness in all the animals (2 Kings 2.19-22). Other miracles he prayed for include how he responded to the widow woman whose sons were threatened to be taken and she had no money. Elisha instructed her to obtain containers to put oil in and they were filled and filled until she had enough money to pay her debt, save her sons, and all live on. Abundance! (2 Kings 4.2-7)

    Elisha also prayed for a woman to have a child when she was barren, that died, and he prayer for the boy to live again (2 Kings 4.36. He fed others in famine (2 Kings 4.38), and he gave the Word of God to Naaman to be cleansed from leprosy (2 Kings 5.10) Another of my very favorite passages talks of how Elisha was so close to God and aware of His presence and protection that he prayed for his servant's eyes to be open to see the whole Host of Heaven gathered to fight for the man of God against an army of attackers. (2 Kings 6.15-17)

    One of my new favorites is when a man who was cutting trees lost his ax-head in the nearby water. 'The man of God said, 'Where did it fall?' When shown the place, Elisha cut off a stick and threw it in there, and the iron floated." (2 Kings 6.6)

    The iron floated. This is impossible. It defies all the laws of physics, but the man of God never saw *anything* too hard for his God. No doubt, no hesitation. I want to see my God the same way Elisha saw his God - our same God. He was not stumped by a heavy metal ax that would NEVER float without the God he served making it float. The ax-head was hopelessly lost and contrary to all expectation, it floated because the things that are impossible with man are possible with God. (Mark 10.27)

God can fix anything - finances, addiction, depression, family turmoil, broken relationships and marriages, hard hearts opposing God - and you name it, He can do it.

Write how you feel your faith meter is. Do you or someone you know need Jesus to fix something?
_____
_____
_____
_____
_____
_____
_____
_____
_____
_____
_____
_____
_____
_____
_____
_____
_____
_____
_____
_____

Day 2 – Trust

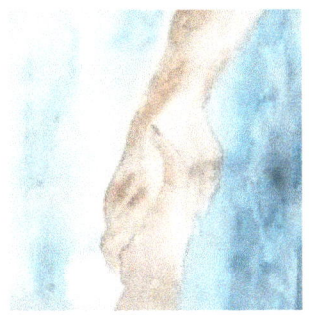

Trust - means to rely on the integrity, strength, ability, and surety of a person or things; confidence. I don't think any being has these qualities more than the Living God.

Trust is something God asks us to do. Trust Him. But trust has always been a difficult thing for me. I feel I should be in control and able to do things in my own strength. Truth is, I think control is an illusion. Who is ever truly in control? Storms hit, earthquakes happen, wars shatter our lives at times, accidents and illness occur at any moment of any day and more. I have control over some things, but for the most part, I think I have no control over the many things that can and do happen every day.

For many years, I had personal struggle with Proverbs 3.5-6. It was just me because I can see the words are lovely, but for some reason, I interpreted them as words that required something I was unable to do. The bottom line is I just had difficulty trusting God and I knew it, just did not want to admit it.

Then, one day, a Pastor made these words gold to me. He said, "Proverbs 3.5-6 tells us to 'Lean on, trust in, *and* be confident in the Lord with all your heart *and* mind and do not rely on your own insight *or* understanding. In all your ways know, recognize, *and* acknowledge Him, and He will direct *and* make straight *and* plain your paths.'"

I had heard the words for many years, but what he said about them is what made it possible for me to do what they exhort me to. He said, "What God is saying is that we do not have to understand how He is going to do what He promises to do, we just give everything to Him. He knows we do not have the strength or ability to figure everything out, but He does and will."

These words melted my cold, unbelieving, untrusting heart and allowed me to see that God is not asking me to understand, but to know He does and that He is able to make the impossible happen, get me through every difficult moment, make a way where there looks like there is no way, heal me, care for me, guide me, and love me with an everlasting love. He is even able to give me the ability to trust Him.

One devotional encouraged me as it said, "You can trust the Man Who died for you." I still struggle with trust at times and will be the first to admit I allow myself to become frightened of circumstances, but am making every effort to trust in God for everything every day.

Write how you feel about how you trust God.

Day 3 - Teacher

I have a substitute teacher's license and have enjoyed teaching the children all their various subjects. To be honest, the younger the age, the more fun it has been to teach. Once, while teaching 1st grade, I told one little girl how smart she was. She asked, "Smarter than you?" I told her I would have to get back to her on that one.

I laugh, but sometimes I also think I am smarter than I really am. Sadly enough, sometimes I even think I am smarter than God. I claim I would do things differently and would have set things up differently and would never let anyone suffer, get sick, or lose people they love. But I find myself humbled because I am not smarter than anyone, especially God. He reminds me of His Greatness in Job 38 and on:

"And now, finally, God answered Job from the eye of a violent storm. He said: "Why do you....talk without knowing what you're talking about? Pull yourself together, Job! Up on your feet! Stand tall! I have some questions for you, and I want some straight answers. Where were you when I created the earth? ...Who decided on its size? .... Are you the one who gave the horse his prowess and adorned him with a shimmering mane? ....Was it through your know-how that the hawk learned to fly, soaring effortlessly on thermal updrafts? Did you command the eagle's flight, and teach her to build her nest in the heights, ..."

God continues for chapters talking about all the things He has created and watches over and the truth is that I have never done anything to create anything on earth. I am just a child of God here and enjoying His grace and presence in my life and all the beauty of His creation. And I need a Teacher.

Knowing my need, God has promised to be my Teacher. (Isaiah 28.26) I am trying to be a good student and know that He is always kind and loving and in control and never makes mistakes. I make many mistakes. The little picture for today - "I wish my Teacher knew..." The truth is my Teacher does know. He teaches us about His love and His nature and how to behave in this world towards others. He teaches about grace and mercy and about our battles in life. He even answers most of my questions when I ask with a sincere desire to understand. Our Teacher knows all about our frailty, our weakness, our pain, our confusion, our inability to comprehend at times, and all about our needs.

Keeping my spirit in a teachable posture is my goal at all times.

Write how you allow God to teach you and how He does teach you every day.

Day 4 – Not Trifle

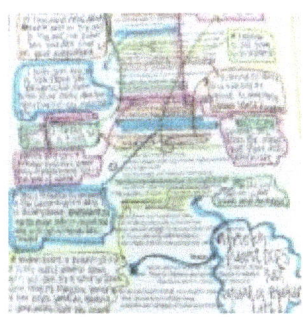

I have a very good friend who has a Bible marked just like the one in this blog today. I remember when I first saw it, I wondered how she managed to circle and underline every single verse with a different color and still manage to find a verse she wanted to find. Some should 'highlight' their 'highlights!' (chuckle)

The person who owns this Bible not only circled and underlined and highlighted verses, they added notes in the margins - to emphasize the amazing Words of the Living God. I am impressed.

This little picture and my friend's Bible show me how special the Word of God is to some people. Every time they find a verse it thrills their heart and they are compelled to make it stand out. I have highlighted many areas in my Bible as well - perhaps not as much as some others - but I do hold so many scriptures close to my heart. I read one Bible so much it was in about 17 sections and I still have all the parts and pieces; but was teased about the condition of that Bible for many years as I brought it with me wherever I went.

This year I decided to read through the entire Bible in one year. Yeah! But not always. I find myself rushing through some chapters because it has become 'just another thing on my already overbooked list' of things to do. I have apologized to God for taking my Bible reading time so lightly and each time I open my Bible, I pray for Him to show me something new and wonderful in His Word - something to underline and highlight.

I love the Words in Deuteronomy 32.46-47 that tell me to "set your [minds and] hearts on all the words which I command you this day, that you may command them to your children, that they may be watchful to do all the words of this law. For it is not an empty *and* worthless trifle for you; it is your [very] life..." God's Word is not trifle, it is my very life. I truly believe this.

I know we all know the familiar Word - "God's Word is a lamp to our feet and a light to our path." - Psalm 119.105. God's Word has the answers to everything we need today and every day.

John 1.1 and 14 tells me "In the beginning was the Word, and the Word was with God, and the Word was God.... the Word became flesh and made His dwelling among us... We have seen His glory, the glory of the One and Only Son, who came from the Father, full of grace and truth." There are three that bear record in heaven - the Father, the Word

(Jesus), and the Holy Spirit; and these are One." (1 John 5.7)

Matthew 24.35 also reminds me that Jesus said, "Heaven and earth will pass away, but My Words will never pass away."

The Word of God is not trifle, it is our very life! Jesus is the Word. I love the Word.

Write how you cherish God's Word and how you read daily.

_____
_____
_____
_____
_____
_____
_____
_____
_____
_____
_____
_____
_____
_____
_____
_____
_____
_____
_____
_____
_____
_____
_____

Day 5 – Talents

    I have always wondered what my particular talents are. I do not play a sport well or a musical instrument well enough to play for others. I love art and dance; but can see natural talent in others that I wish I myself had. I think talents can be skills as well as money.

    Matthew 25 tells the parable of Jesus giving talents - to one person He gave 1 talent, to another 2 talents, another 5 and one He gave 10 talents. This has always led me to believe that Christians have been given different talents and some have more responsibility because the Bible also tells me that to whom much is given, much is required. (Luke 12.48)

    This takes me back to 'What are my talents?' I am still not so sure, but I was talking with a friend and I told her how I sort of laughed when I thought 'could it be possible for someone to have been given 'no' talents?' I told her I could not think of my own particular talent/s but I have some loved ones that I think others may consider without any particular talent in life. What about them?

My friend's husband has a relative that struggled with schizophrenia all his life. He was not functional in society, but seemed better when he was given medication. He recently passed away and my friend wondered what purpose a life like his is to this world? The bottom line is 'what was/is he worth?'

I realize this world puts emphasis on success and talents and, while I do not diminish the importance of success and talents being utilized, I think there are some people with little or possibly no apparent talents. Perhaps I just do not recognize some peoples' talents.

Does that make the ones with fewer or apparently no talents less valuable? NO! I am convinced that the Living God loves them more than I can imagine. Their small lives that may amount to nothing in my eyes or the world's eyes do matter and are highly valued by the Father.

One of my brothers died forty years ago when he was twenty years old. I was unprepared to experience this. I prayed and asked God where my brother was for eternity because I never heard him make a 'profession of faith.' I remember God's answer to this day.

God said, "Blessed are the poor in spirit, for theirs is the Kingdom of God.' (Matthew 5.3) and He also said, "The least on this earth will be the greatest in the Kingdom of God." (Mark 10.31 Living Bible) My brother was seen and known by the God I love. God did not miss my brother's life and value and he has been with the King for many years and is the greatest in the Kingdom of God even though he was unnoticed here on earth and had no great accomplishments in his life.

Throughout the Bible, the God of the Universe reminds me how important each and every one of us are. He even counts the hairs on our heads. (Matthew 10.30) And the truth that "God so loved the world, He gave His Only Son, so that whoever believes on Him, shall never perish, but have everlasting life' (John 3.16) will always be true for all of us.

Write how you find your talents and realize how you can use them for God and how you are valuable to God just because you are His._____

_____
_____
_____
_____
_____
_____
_____
_____
_____
_____
_____
_____
_____
_____
_____
_____

Day 6 – Pierce My Ear

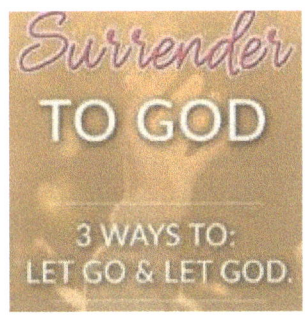

I must admit, surrender is not an easy thing for me. In fact, when I read verses like Isaiah 64.8 'Yet, O Lord, You are our Father; we are the clay, and You our Potter, and we all are the work of Your hand' and Jeremiah 18.6 'O house of Israel, can I not do with you as this potter does? says the Lord. Behold, as the clay is in the potter's hand, so are you in My hand,' I would cringe deep inside.

My mental images tended toward torture and crushing me to smithereens. Smithereens is a funny word - 'broken into small bits or pieces.' It all had to do with my concept of God. I did not see Him working on my heart to my benefit and I never saw Him as liking who I was and 'changing' me meant I was defective - the way I was afraid I was. All this twisted thinking did a real number on my ability to surrender to the Living God and truly trust Him and love Him. I would think 'do anything but hurt me please.'

Well, it has been many years of patience on the part of the Living God to help me to surrender and help me to trust. In fact, one author helped me see that God really does like the 'me' He created and wants me to be that 'me.' Surrender means that the more I abandon the clamor of self-will, the more I become that 'me' He created as I surrender to Him.

One of my favorite parts of the Bible is Deuteronomy 15.12- 17. While I do not understand all the customs of other cultures or long ago, sometimes it seemed safer and wiser to be under someone's umbrella of protection, but it meant being a 'servant.' Deuteronomy talks about what to do with those who have been in this position.

'If any of your people ... sell themselves to you and serve you six years, in the seventh year you must let them go free. And when you release them, do not send them away empty-handed. Supply them liberally from your flock, your threshing floor and your winepress. Give to them as the Lord your God has blessed you. Remember that you were slaves in Egypt and the Lord your God redeemed you. That is why I give you this command today.' It touches my heart how God commands for generosity and supply to those less fortunate.

But, the next part is especially touching - 'But if your servant says to you, "I do not want to leave you," because he loves you and your family and is well off with you, then take an awl and push it through his earlobe into the door, and he will become your servant for life.'

I have come to the place in life, by the grace of God, that I do not want to leave Him, I love Him; and I want Him to:

Pierce my ear, O Lord my God
Lead me to Your door this day
I will serve no other gods
Lord, I'm here to stay
For You have paid the price for me
With Your blood, You ransomed me
I will serve you eternally
A free man I'll never be.

I will be a willing bond servant to Jesus forever.

Write how you feel your commitment to God and His will are.

_____
_____
_____
_____
_____
_____
_____
_____
_____
_____
_____
_____
_____
_____
_____
_____

Day 7 – 911

I was an ambulance driver in Cleveland, Ohio for three years when I was a young woman. I learned that one really needs to keep a serious outlook on many things, but a sense of humor really helps as well.

On occasion, the dispatching team shared stories about the incoming phone calls they received from the public. I realize their job can be very stressful at times, but I am certain all the 911 call receivers agree that not taking everything too seriously helps them do their jobs well.

Recently, my sister and I were talking. She works with the elderly in a nursing home and told me one of the resident's family called 911 because they could not find their parent's dentures. I was a little disgusted and said, "You can't call 911 for lost items." My sister proceeded to give me an education in Georgia 911 calls. She said, "We have residents call 911 all the time. They call and say they need a bedpan..." That's when I began to laugh hysterically. I immediately heard the 911 operator say, "911- what's your emergency?' to receive "I need the bedpan" at the other end. Even though it is pretty sad when the elderly may not be able to get staff to respond to them and they resort to calling for help - any help - even 911, wouldn't you just love to be the 911 operator for that call? We must have laughed for 20 minutes thinking of this. She said she felt all the cell phones should be taken from the residents. We laughed more.

My sister said the 911 dispatchers call the home to inform them of the call and ask if the staff will handle the call. Problem solved, no charges filed. No harm done.

I remember how I chuckled when I first read Psalm 44.23-36. The children of Israel were in distress and it seems like the 911 verse of the Bible - 'Awake! Why do You sleep, O Lord? Arouse Yourself, cast us not off forever! Why do You hide Your face *and* forget our affliction and our oppression? For our lives are bowed down to the dust; our bodies cleave to the ground. Rise up! Come to our help, and deliver us for Your mercy's sake *and* because of Your steadfast love!'

They sound pretty desperate. I know I have and have made 911 calls to God on more than one occasion. He is a very present help in time of need. He will respond. (Psalm 46.1) Even though I think He has forgotten, decided not to, out helping someone else, very slow, and more, He is on the job and will help.

Psalm 121 encourages me. "I will lift up mine eyes unto the hills, from where comes my help. My help comes from the Lord, Who made heaven and earth. He will not suffer thy foot to be moved: He that keeps you will not slumber. Behold, he that keeps Israel shall neither slumber nor sleep. The Lord is thy keeper: the Lord is thy shade upon thy right hand. The sun shall not smite thee by day, nor the moon by night. The Lord shall preserve thee from all evil: he shall preserve thy soul. The Lord shall preserve thy going out and thy coming in from this time forth, and even for evermore.'

We have His Word on it. He will help. He does not sleep or slumber. He is always working and always talking.

We can call on Him anytime and in any emergency!

Do you call on God in emergency situations? Write how you ask God for help for yourself and your loved ones.

_____
_____
_____
_____
_____
_____
_____
_____
_____
_____
_____

Day 8 – All things

I don't know about everyone else, but I have had some very challenging times. One year had mixed feelings about being relieved a particular year was over and being happy for all that happened. Between work and family and new business ventures and more! Some years are very busy.

Some years have had some great moments, but also moments of loss. I am sure everyone has experienced similar things. I lost a very dear friend one year. I know she is with the Savior and looks down on me and smiles, but I sure do miss her. Also made some great new memories, new friends, and new opportunities have come my way.

There were many times I thought I was in way over my head and did not handle every situation well. I shared struggles with close friends; and we prayed. One night, while sharing some concerns, the Lord spoke to my heart and the words, 'I can do all things through Christ Who strengthens me' (Philippians 4.13) poured from my lips.

It was amazing the impact these words had on my heart and my circumstances. I have read that verse for over forty years and now, in my time of need, it is here to comfort and encourage me. I have quoted it every time I thought things were getting too difficult to handle. They broke any spirits of defeat or discouragement inside and truly God gave me strength to manage every situation.

The Bible is filled with encouragement for all our needs and challenges. Romans 8.37 wonderfully tells us 'Nay, in all these things we are more than conquerors through him that loved us.' MORE than a conqueror. 1 Corinthians 15.57 also assures us '..thanks be to God, which giveth us the victory through our Lord Jesus Christ.' Victory over loss, heartache, oppression, lack, anything.

We all have New Years to celebrate and I know I need to look to the Lord for His strength each day. Whatever I face, I can do all things through Christ Who strengthens me.

I love the words to Steven Curtis Chapman's song "His Strength Is Perfect"

I can do all things
Through Christ who gives me strength
But sometimes I wonder
what He can do through me
No great success to show
No glory on my own
Yet in my weakness He is there to let me know

His strength is perfect when our strength is gone
He'll carry us when we can't carry on
Raised in His power, the weak become strong
His strength is perfect, His strength is perfect
We can only know
The power that He holds
When we truly see how deep our weakness goes
His strength in us begins
Where ours comes to an end
He hears our humble cry and proves again

His strength is perfect when our strength is gone
He'll carry us when we can't carry on
Raised in His power, the weak become strong
His strength is perfect, His strength is perfect

Write how you look forward to God's strength and blessings in each new year and each day.

_____
_____
_____
_____
_____
_____
_____
_____
_____
_____
_____
_____
_____
_____
_____
_____
_____
_____

Day 9 – The Ultimate Gift

I always have at least one person on my list at Christmas that I never know what present to buy them. This person seems to have everything they need; and I joke about just getting them 'more of everything they already have.' But the challenge continues each year.

I am blessed and have been given much by God. I do not give Him Christmas gifts, but if I did, I feel stumped. I ask myself, 'What can I give God?' Many wonder why I would ask that because usually He is the Giver of all good things. (James 1.17). And, the Word tells us that 'the Earth is the Lord's and everything that's in it' (Psalm 24.1) and that 'He owns all the cattle on a thousand hills.' (Psalm 50.10)

So, God really is the One Being that has everything. He does not *need* anything. To be honest, I never think I have anything that could be good enough to give to God. I have flaws and failures and broken dreams and futile attempts at walking the line most days. What could I possibly give to the God of the Universe that would matter?

But that being said, there is something He really wants us to give Him. When I was a young girl being pursued by the Living God, I heard Him speak to my heart one night. He said, "Give me your heart." I was frightened because I did not know Who He was or What He was and did not realize I could trust Him and I did not realize how much He loved me and wanted great things for me.

It took me about one year of being pursued by God to want to give Him my heart as He asks us to do in Proverbs 23.26. I feel this is the ultimate gift that gives the Father pleasure - to have us be His children - to have His sheep know His voice, follow Him, and trust Him with their hearts and lives and everything every day. He treasures the gift of our hearts. It's not what He *needs*, it's what He *wants*.

I recently learned that the composer (Hugh Martin) of 'Have Yourself a Merry Little Christmas' also had these words to that tune --

Have yourself a blessed little Christmas
Christ the King is born
Let your voices ring upon this happy morn

Have yourself a blessed little Christmas
Serenade the Earth
Tell the world we celebrate the Savior's birth

Let us all proclaim the joyous tidings
Voices raised on high

Send this carol soaring up into the sky,
This very merry blessed Christmas lullaby.

Let us gather to sing to Him
And to bring to Him our praise
Son of God and a Friend of all
To the end of all our days

Sings hosannas, hymns, and hallelujahs
As to Him we bow
Make the music mighty as the heav'ns allow
And have yourself a blessed little Christmas now.

Write how you feel you have given your heat to God and how you celebrate the Savior each Advent season.

_____
_____
_____
_____
_____
_____
_____
_____
_____
_____
_____
_____
_____
_____
_____
_____
_____

Day 10 – Sharing – Just Like A Child

A time for giving

Dad and I liked to watch world news with David Muir each evening. I have never been a news buff because all the news seems like 'bad' news and never 'good' news, but David Muir always has something sweet at the end of his news.

During Halloween, he had a story about a little boy trick-or-treating. The young boy came to a home with a pumpkin basket on the porch; but there was no more candy in the pumpkin. The little boy informed his mom of the situation. It seemed he had a problem. At first, I wondered what he would do. Then, to my surprise - to fix it, he proceeded to take candy from his bag and put it into the empty pumpkin basket on the porch. Problem solved - the pumpkin basket was no longer empty. The sweetest thing is that he did not know anyone was watching, but this was all captured on the home security camera and that is how all of us in news land were able to see the kindness, sweetness, and innocence of this young man. I was touched once again that good things do happen every day.

I am called to be like a child. Even though seasons come and seasons go, I can turn my heart to how I can fill up someone's basket that is empty. God promises that it is impossible to out-give Him.

I am first reminded in James 1.17 that, "every good gift and every perfect gift is from above, and comes down from the Father of lights.." Our Heavenly Father gives great gifts.

My motive, however, should be pure - just for the sake of sharing with others less fortunate, however, God's Word promises - "Give, and [gifts] will be given to you; good measure, pressed down, shaken together, and running over, will they pour into [the pouch formed by] the bosom [of your robe and used as a bag]. For with the measure you deal out [with the measure you use when you confer benefits on others], it will be measured back to you." (Luke 6.38) I believe His promise of 'pressed down, shaken together, and running over' is to me and the ones I love and bless.

Genesis 9.3 lets me know that "(God) give(s) ... everything." And Proverbs 28.27 tells me, "He who gives to the poor will not want." God's Word is clear - He is a giver and I, as His child am to be a giver too - with the spirit that shows how grateful I am that God has given to me.

Luke 12.32 warms my heart with the words, "Fear not, little flock; for it is your Father's good pleasure to give you the kingdom." The Kingdom is Him and His salvation, goodness, faithfulness, provision, answers to prayer, and everything I have here and in my heart.

God Bless you all Seasons. I hope you find someone to bless.

Write about how you share your blessing with others. What do you have to give?

Day 11 – Seeds

I am always amazed at how one small seed, planted in the ground, can cause a plant to grow and produce so much. From apples on an apple tree to corn on the stalk, it all begins with little seeds.

Genesis 1.29 tells us how God gave us seeds as a gift - "and God said, See, I have given you every plant yielding seed that is on the face of all the land and every tree with seed in its fruit; you shall have them for food." Our Provider is incredible beyond words.

The cycle of life is wonderful to me. The fruit and vegetables we enjoy are not only grown in abundance, they carry with them more seeds for planting and harvesting even more fruit and vegetables. God's supply is generous and 'superabundantly above all that we could ask or think.' (Ephesians 3.20)

God tells us about seeds:

"...Isaac sowed seed in that land and received in the same year a hundred times as much as he had planted, and the Lord favored him with blessings. (Genesis 26.12) God multiples our fruits and vegetables and He multiples His spiritual blessings to us as well.

God tells us not to judge a seed by its size:

"Of all the seeds (the mustard seed) is the smallest, but when it has grown it is the largest of the garden herbs and becomes a tree, so that the birds of the air come and find shelter in its branches, but look what it brings!" (Matthew 13.32)

And He also mentions the mustard seed in comparison to how much faith it takes for us to pray and believe and receive, "He said to them, ... if you have faith ... like a grain of mustard seed, you can say to this mountain, move from here to yonder place, and it will move; and *nothing* will be impossible to you." (Matthew 17.20) Doesn't seem like it takes much faith much to make great things happen.

Jesus spoke of the Word being like seeds in our hearts:

"But as for that [seed] in the good soil, these are [the people] who, hearing the Word, hold it fast in a just (noble, virtuous) and worthy heart, and steadily bring forth fruit with patience." (Luke 8.15) God wants His Word to take root and grow and flourish in our hearts.

God wants us to use seed to win others for the Kingdom:

"...he who goes forth bearing seed and weeping ... shall doubtless come again with rejoicing, bringing his sheaves with him." (Psalms 126.6) This is a very old-time way of speaking of winning souls for Christ.

Everyone plays a part:

"I (Paul) planted, Apollos watered, but God [all the while] was making it grow *and* [He] gave the increase." (1 Corinthians 3.6). Our efforts are never 'fruitless' because God is the Force behind all our efforts and He never loses and nothing is ever wasted.

It is true, seeds are small. Sometimes we see our gifts as small, but God takes those gifts and causes them to grow. What we need to do is sow our seeds. Our seeds of kindness, a smile, a word of encouragement, a meal, a token of appreciation, supporting a good cause, listening to ones who need us to listen, sitting by the beds of our friends and family when life is changing from earth to heaven, and more. Every day, we have seeds to sow and give to others. We may not always see the reward here or visibly see how we touched someone's life, but we have God's word on the matter, that what we do, He will make matter. Some of us plant, some of us water, but it is God that gives the blessing and increase! We can sow a lot of seeds.

Write how you feel God sees you and how you use your gifts for others.

Day 12 –Always Thankful

I love Thanksgiving. It is not only a time for special thanks and turkey and family, it means Christmas is very near again. YEAH! I titled this 'Always Thanksgiving' because, while we have *one* day we *call* Thanksgiving, the truth is that every day is a time for giving thanks.

I think being thankful is another way I give praise to God and acknowledge Him as great and as my Lord and show Him I believe He is good and providing for me at all times, even if it is not exactly what I had in mind.

There have been times it was difficult to be thankful. I have been jobless, homeless, foodless, hopeless, on the verge of losing everything, and wondered why and how these things happened in my lifetime. Recovery is great, but when going through the valley of the shadow of death (Psalm 23.4), thanks is not the first impulse in my heart.

God's Word tell me to "Thank God in everything - no matter what the circumstances may be, be thankful and give thanks, for this is the will of God for you who are in Christ Jesus - the Revealer and Mediator of that will. (1 Thessalonians 5.18) and that "...all things work together for good to them that love God..." (Romans 8.28) So, if I really take God at His Word, then He knows everything and will make even the things I think are really bad turn out for good. It has taken some time to work these truths into my life.

One of my favorite movies is *Pollyanna*. In the movie, she is a 12-year-old orphaned daughter of missionaries who came to live with her rich and strict aunt. Pollyanna is a very cheerful, talkative and radically optimistic youngster who focuses on the goodness of life and always finds something to be glad about, no matter the situation. She plays the 'glad game.' The game is where - no matter what is happening - you find one thing to be glad about. Once she had a broken leg. When she played the glad game, she was glad to have crutches.

I think I should have no difficulty finding more than one thing to be thankful for each day and in each circumstance. I have Jesus as my Savior, family, all my friends, I live in a free country, I can pray, I have a Bible, I have a home now, and many more blessing each and every day. Now I have enough to share with others too. I want to always find something to be thankful for and meditate on that each day to help me walk through all the good and bad times of life. I am thankful for everything. I pray you are too.

Write how you are thankful each day.

Day 13 - Filled

I love pastry. One of my favorite things is crème-filled donuts. The more cream the better. "Fill them up," I say. While donuts are not great for my weight watcher's diet, I love chocolate or vanilla crème just the same.

The Bible talks about being filled - not with vanilla or chocolate crème though. It's my spirit that needs filled. I know my spiritual tank feels like it is running on empty so much of the time. God knows when I am a little less patient, a little less kind, a little less thoughtful, a little less generous, etc. I think those times are because I am a little less 'filled.' My tank is on empty and I need a refill. Sooooo, I know I need to spend time in the Word and in prayer and fellowship with God.

One of my many favorite sections of the Bible is the wonderful prayer for all of us in Ephesians 3.16-19

"May He grant you out of the rich treasury of His glory to be strengthened *and* reinforced with mighty power in the inner man by the [Holy] Spirit [Himself indwelling your innermost being and personality].

May Christ through your faith [actually] dwell (settle down, abide, make His permanent home) in your hearts! May you be rooted deep in love *and* founded securely on love,

That you may have the power *and* be strong to apprehend *and* grasp with all the saints [God's devoted people, the experience of that love] what is the breadth and length and height and depth [of it];

[That you may really come] to know [practically, through experience for yourselves] the love of Christ, which far surpasses mere knowledge [without experience]; that you may be filled [through all your being] unto all the fullness of God [may have the richest measure of the divine Presence, and become a body wholly filled and flooded with God Himself]!"

Filled with God Himself! What a wonderful privilege to know that God does not just want to give me a little of Himself; but wants me to be filled with Him and to really know His love. When I am filled with God, my tank is full; and I am able to be more of what He wants me to be and give from a full tank - so to speak.

There is no end to God's supply - He tells me "the Earth is the Lord's and the fullness thereof" (Psalm 24.1) and that He "owns the cattle on a thousand hills." (Psalm 50.10)

God wants to fill us with His provision as well as His love, His mercy, His goodness, His patience, His kindness, His Presence and everything about Himself. He wants us to know personally what He is all about and His great love.

Meditate on how you view God and His abundance and being filled with Him.

_____
_____
_____
_____
_____
_____
_____
_____
_____
_____
_____
_____
_____
_____
_____
_____
_____
_____
_____
_____
_____
_____
_____
_____

Day 14 – Perspective

There are many ways to think about trees. Some feel trees are spectacular parts of nature, but others consider them a nuisance because they either want to make room for other things or they fall down on precious property with weather or aging conditions. Others look at trees as providers of shade on warm days or as very fun to climb or hang a swing from or put a tree house in for play. Some use trees for art and change the direction of the growth to provide unusual and artistic forms to the trees. I have seen this in Key West as well as many Asian countries.

In addition, some feel trees are home to many birds and small critters like squirrels and, my personal favorite, at the Cologne Zoo in Germany, fun for the elephants starts after the holidays because they are fed all the unsold Christmas trees - soooo, the elephants see the tree as a delicious snack!

Where am I going with this? Well, I think life is a matter of perspective - not only about trees, but I also relate this to my difficulties. Most of the time,

I see my trials as the worst thing that could ever happen to me and wish difficulties never happened. If I change my perspective just a tad - a major over hall for me - perhaps I can see them differently. I have decided that I need to turn every worry, job loss, brothers and sisters struggling, car keys being locked in the truck, loss of health or a loved one, and all the other little things on my 'what can go wrong today' list into an opportunity to see the greatness of God. I want to see for myself His faithfulness, kindness, love and care, and attention to every little detail in my life.

I admit that I have never been fond of James 1.2-4 - "Consider it wholly joyful, my brethren, whenever you are enveloped in *or* encounter trials of any sort *or* fall into various temptations. Be assured *and* understand that the trial *and* proving of your faith bring out endurance *and* steadfastness *and* patience. But let endurance *and* steadfastness *and* patience have full play *and* do a thorough work, so that you may be [people] perfectly and fully developed [with no defects], lacking in nothing."

God's Word goes on to promise, "If anyone lacks wisdom, let him ask God ... and it will be given..." I sure do need wisdom, so I ask the Father for wisdom about how to view the daily struggles and how to see Him in everything.

Proverbs 24.20 tells me always that "(my) steps are ordered by the Lord." He is in control of the Universe, but He is also in control of every step

I take. Even if I think I have taken a bad one, He makes my "crooked paths straight." (Isaiah 42.16)

I also have the assurance that "God has said, 'I will not in any way fail you *nor* give you up *nor* leave you without support. [I will] not, [I will] not, [I will] not in any degree leave you helpless *nor* forsake *nor* let [you] down relax My hold on you)! Assuredly not!'" (Hebrews 13.5) Amen.

Write how you feel about trials and God's presence in them.

_____
_____
_____
_____
_____
_____
_____
_____
_____
_____
_____
_____
_____
_____
_____
_____
_____
_____
_____
_____
_____
_____

Day 15 – Never Cease

I love pandas. They are really cute. This one looks to me like he is praying, so I included him here today. He reminds me of what I need to be doing more and more of.

I feel like I am not alone in forgetting to pray. When I have a problem or feel I am lacking in something, I do everything except pray. The other day I was driving to work on a road we should have been able to go at least 60 mph on and, instead, I was forced to drive down the road at 45-50 mph for over 20 miles. Now, I realize I am in need of patience, however, I informed God that I did not want any lessons on the road this day. Needless to say, I received the memo from heaven that told me, 'It's either His way, or it's His way.' I tried to say, 'No thank you' to the lesson today, but, needless to say again, that did not work.

So, I decided God wanted to slow me down and He wanted me to pray. I did. I spent the extra time on the road going through my list of personal prayers and prayers for family and friends that are so dear to me. I was also able to enjoy a radio teaching about prayer as well and was reminded how Apostle Paul never ceased praying.

"For this reason, we also, from the day we heard of it, have not ceased to pray *and* make [special] request for you, [asking] ..."(Colossians 1.9)

I was challenged to wonder if there is there anything in my life I value enough to never cease praying for. I am convicted of my lack of persistence in prayer for loved ones who - years later - still struggle. I know God has not given up on them and I need to remind myself to not give up on them or answers to my own prayers that have gone unanswered for many years.

I read one man's devotion that said, "The devil is not troubled when ... writes books or prepares sermons, but his knobby knees tremble when ... prays. The devil does not stutter or stumble when you walk through church doors or attend committee meetings.....But the walls of hell shake when one person with an honest heart and faithful confession prays and also says, "Oh, God, how great Thou art.""

The devil keeps us from prayer. He tries to come between us and God and fill our hearts and minds with doubts and business that hinders us. But he scampers like a spooked dog when we pray. So let's do.

Let's pray, *first*. Traveling to help the hungry? Be sure to bathe your mission in prayer. Working to disentangle the knots of injustice? Pray. Weary with a world of racism and division? So is God. And He would love to talk to you about it.

Let's pray, *most*. Did God call us to preach without ceasing? Or teach without ceasing? Or have committee meetings without ceasing? Or sing without ceasing? No, but He did call us to "pray without ceasing." (1 Thessalonians 5.17)

Let's pray.

Write how you feel your prayer life is growing and what you can do to make it better.

_____
_____
_____
_____
_____
_____
_____
_____
_____
_____
_____
_____
_____
_____
_____
_____
_____
_____
_____
_____

Day 16 – Tombstone

I think - that most think - talking about death is morbid. And I do think so - if I must say so - myself. There are times I am convinced that I will live forever - not only in heaven, but here on Earth. I am wrong; I do realize.

I recently found some tombstones I viewed funny though. One tombstone my brother and I found in a cemetery in Key West said, "I told you I was sick." We laughed together reading it and he identified with that one because he was sick and no one seemed to realize it. He has since passed. He told us he was sick!

The stones I viewed ranged from funny to really funny stuff about a not so funny topic. Another I recently viewed said, "Don't laugh, you're next." Others said, "Myra Mains," "Here lays my husband, Tom.. Now I know where he is at night," "Buttermilk Hatfield - Tried milkin' a cow that was really a bull, Milk can's empty, grave is full," and "Ben Better" to share a few.

If the stone in the blog is difficult to read, it says 'Here he lies, but he never died!' Praise God. That is one thing I think I would like on my tombstone. We never die when we know Jesus. If Jesus left the grave behind Him, so will I. During devotions one day, I read someone else's thoughts. He said:

"Recently I discovered it's possible to record a message for my tombstone. And if I do, this may be what you'll hear:

Thanks for coming by. Sorry you missed me, but I'm not here. I'm home. Finally home! At some point my King will call, and this grave will be shown for the temporary tomb it is. You might want to step to the side in case that happens while you are here. Hope you've made plans for your own departure. All the best, ... "

I am in the position - like so many others - of impending loss and having had much loss already in life. Sometimes I think life is all about loss. I, like most, like to avoid the very sad topic of departing to heaven and, even though this should be a celebrated event, it does not seem to be.

Psalms 116.15 assures us, "Precious (important and no light matter) in the sight of the Lord is the death of His saints (His loving ones)."

Jesus has promised, "I am [Myself] the Resurrection and the Life. Whoever believes in (adheres to, trusts in, and relies on) Me, although he may die, yet he shall live" (John 11.25) and it will be with Him in Paradise. (Luke 23.43)

I would like to say, "I can't wait!" but I think I want to wait until the Lord calls me home. For the ones I am walking with along their long and winding roads that are leading this way, I pray for the words to comfort them and assure them that Jesus is waiting for them and it will be great! He promised.

Write how you feel about seeing Jesus and others that have gone before us.

_____
_____
_____
_____
_____
_____
_____
_____
_____
_____
_____
_____
_____
_____
_____
_____
_____
_____
_____
_____
_____

Day 17 – Lazarus, Mary, Martha and Me

Anyone who has ever read my blogs knows I have a million favorite parts of my Bible. Another one is the account of Jesus raising Lazarus from the dead in John 11. While the account itself is amazing and beyond words, I love the details in the middle of the story. Mary and Martha.

We all know the account - Jesus hears Lazarus is not well. He intentionally does not respond quickly. Lazarus dies. Jesus arrives at the home of Lazarus and his sisters, Mary and Martha. When the girls hear Jesus has arrived, they are so distressed they begin to say some things we may consider objectionable. Martha says, "Master, if You had been here, my brother would not have died." (v.21) When I read this, I can only imagine her grief and how upset she was and essentially said, "If You were here, doing something to help us, being the Friend you are to us and the Jesus we know You to be - my brother would not have died.

The terrible thing that has happened would not have happened."

It is Jesus' response that melts my heart. He never scolds her or tells what her problems are and how little faith she has or how dare her accuse Him in any way of not caring. I can hear His soft, sweet, kind voice say, "Your brother shall rise again." (v. 23)

Some in the crowd made similar accusations - "Could not He Who opened the eyes of the blind man have kept this man from dying?" (v. 37)

Then Jesus wonders where Mary is. When she comes, same thing - "When Mary reached the place where Jesus was and saw him, she fell at his feet and said, 'Lord, if you had been here, my brother would not have died.'" (v. 32) Then, our wonderful Savior, does not scold her either or wonder if there is any faith to be had anywhere. He is so touched by her crying and grief, He cries too. (v.35)

Just like Mary and Martha and me too - when times are overwhelming and we cannot understand and we are filled with grief and questions and upset, we may wonder about things. But God is right there with us. Holding us in His Everlasting arms. No condemnation; just love. He is still God. He is still good. He is still real. He is still our Father. He will walk through the times with us when we feel the most lost. He will weep with us.

Isaiah 53 reminds us He carries our sorrows and griefs - we do not have to carry them. "Surely

He has borne our griefs (sicknesses, weaknesses, and distresses) and carried our sorrows *and* pains [of punishment], ...He was wounded for our transgressions, He was bruised for our guilt *and* iniquities; the chastisement [needful to obtain] peace *and* well-being for us was upon Him, and with the stripes [that wounded] Him we are healed *and* made whole." (Isaiah 53.4-5)

God understands everything.

Do you have something in life that you need to feel God's understanding about?

_____
_____
_____
_____
_____
_____
_____
_____
_____
_____
_____
_____
_____
_____
_____
_____
_____
_____
_____
_____

18 –Why'd He Do It?

Sometimes, when I have been doing something for a very long time, I get a little stagnant. I hate to admit it's easy for me to just fly through something (like my time with God) without really noticing precious detail and I take things for granted.

There are times, sometimes more than others, it hits me deeply to think about what Jesus did for me. I experience so much strife at times trying to get things done, fighting with family, stressed about a conflict at work, wondering what will happen next in life, will everything work out, will the dog's surgery go well, will I make it thru the week? It's easy for my mind to just sit on that hamster wheel and go round and round. God has such a sweet and gentle way of getting me off that hamster wheel and taking time for cherished moments with Him.

During my devotions recently, I read Ephesians 2. At the beginning of the chapter, I found (for probably the 200th time or more) a list of all the things God has done for me - "and you [He made alive], when you were dead .... God—so rich is He in His mercy! Because of *and* in order to satisfy the great *and* wonderful *and* intense love with which He loved us.. He made us alive together in fellowship *and* in union with Christ; [He gave us the very life of Christ Himself, the same new life with which He quickened Him, for] it is by grace (His favor and mercy which you did not deserve) that you are saved (delivered from judgment and made partakers of Christ's salvation). And He raised us up together with Him and made us sit down together [giving us (joint seating with Him] in the heavenly sphere [by virtue of our being] in Christ Jesus (the Messiah, the Anointed One)."

That's not all He did. He restored me, healed me, makes me His child, gives me the victory, leads me into triumph, makes me more than a conqueror, forgives me everything, provides for me, protects me, directs my every step, and everything more.

Why would He do all these things for me? The astounding and humbling answer comes in verse 7 of Ephesians 2 - "He did this that He might clearly demonstrate through the ages to come the immeasurable (limitless, surpassing) riches of His free grace (His unmerited favor) in His kindness *and* goodness of heart toward us in Christ Jesus."

He did all these things so that He might show me His grace and His kindness to me. His desire is to shower me with love and grace. How undeserving I am to belong to a God Who is so selflessly gracious to me, but I am truly grateful. It is amazing that the

God of the Universe - Who commands waves and watches sparrows and has so much to consider each day, thinks of us and wants to be personal with us.

Write your thoughts about why Jesus sacrificed for you and your loved ones.

Day 19 – The Three O's

Recently, while sharing some of my chaotic life with a friend, we decided I may be taking up all of God's time. We laughed.

The truth is I am pretty needy. On my list today is - I need God to help me get my day started, keep me safe in traffic, give me favor with my employers and customers and help me to do the best I can for the ones I work for and with, make me an example of Christ as much as I am able, open doors to share my faith with others around me, be on the lookout for needs of others I can help with, help me pray for those in need and who need Christ, answer my prayers for my aging mother and father and their health issues and allow me to help them in this season of their lives, keep the siblings and friends I cherish in His hands and care that struggle with addition, heart issues, and other medical and personal concerns, help me walk with my friend through her battle with cancer and end of this life issues, help me find just the right shoes to match my pretty new dress, answer my prayers for employment opportunities for friends and family seeking employment, finding time to talk to lonely friends, helping my new endeavors with publishing my books and my authors' books and knowing which contests to enter and how to be noticed in a noisy world, receiving more creative authors to partner with in publishing their books, finding creative individuals to enhance my authors' work, creating new art work for my card and craft businesses, open doors for marketing my art projects and crafts, providing rest and relaxation and fun in my crazy life, help me with my diet and exercise goals to keep a healthy life, provide the workers to help fix my broken window and fencing, replacing my missing gutters, continue to keep my truck with over 280,000 rolling down the road, give me a hope and a future, guide my every step and more - much, much, much more every day.

Whew! I think I keep God very busy. In fact, my friend and I figured we couldn't see how God has time for anyone else because He is sooooo busy with me and my needs. Funny as we think this is, it is untrue. The Good News is that the Omnipotent (all powerful), Omnipresent (all present), and Omniscient (all knowing) Living God has time for everyone - no matter if they have a list of needs just like mine, a few less, or even more than I have!

God said, "I am the Alpha and Omega, the Beginning and the End... Who is and Who was and Who is to come, the Almighty (the Ruler of all). (Revelation 1.8). He is the God of our past, our present and our future!

And NOTHING is too trivial for God as Job 36.5 tells us - "Behold! God is mighty, and yet despises no one nor regards anything as trivial; He is mighty in power of understanding *and* heart."

Matthew 10.30 reminds us "... the very hairs of your head are all numbered" and Matthew 6.32 assures us, "for your heavenly Father knows that ye have need of all these things."

It is a fact; God has time for everyone. He sees us and is concerned about every little detail of us and our lives.

Write about your needs and tell them to God.

_____
_____
_____
_____
_____
_____
_____
_____
_____
_____
_____
_____
_____
_____
_____
_____
_____
_____
_____
_____

Day 20 – Hope

Have you ever had someone say, "I hope so"? and they didn't mean to, but they said it as if it was last thing in the world they thought would ever happen, but 'they are hoping.'

The Bible tells us there is 'faith, *hope,* and love...' (1 Corinthians 13). There is it - HOPE - along with the other giants of the Bible - LOVE and FAITH. Seems to me that 'hope' gets short changed - hope seems almost flimsy compared to love and faith.

I think hope is one of the most essential things about being human. As a matter of fact, I think only humans are capable of hoping. I think hope is closely bound to faith.

I have been in medicine for over 40 years. I have learned that the one thing I must never do is take away someone's *hope.* Without hope we stop believing something or someone can change, we stop trying to be better or be well, we stop striving to succeed, and, in reality, we give up. What a horrible thing it is to be without hope.

With hope, we see the world as something good and our circumstance as something temporary (hopefully - no pun intended). We see possibilities that are not realized at this particular moment, but that can be. Hope keeps us going and going and going. Hope helps our spirits to be cheerful. I think many find 'hope' something they need to hide because we do not find 'hope' as approving as 'faith.' We all know faith is believing even when all hope is lost or all signs of answer is gone, but hope helps us to continue to travel along in life even when we feel we do not have the faith we wish we did. It's almost like a secret weapon to keep encouraging ourselves. Hope actually improves every area of our lives and helps us to try even when things are difficult.

And our hope is not unfounded, but based on the very Word of God. Romans 15.13 reminds us 'Now the God of hope fill you with all joy and peace in believing, that ye may abound in hope, through the power of the Holy Ghost.'

The God of all hope. The God that knows we need hope. The Giver of all good gifts gives us hope. Zechariah 9.12 calls us 'prisoners of hope.' That ye - meaning 'you' if ye didn't get that - may *abound* in hope. I like that. We have hope. We have God. We can continue on in this life knowing God has given us hope in the midst of any circumstance in our lives, homes, country, or in this unpredictable world.

Write how you will pray to have love and faith today, and also pray for hope.

Day 21 - Fog

I love stories about great men of faith - one of my favorite men of faith is George Mueller. "I believe God..." was the title of the devotion sharing a conversation between another passenger and the captain of a ship that went on to say:

"I went to America some years ago with the captain of a steamer, who was a very devoted Christian. When off the coast of Newfoundland, he said to me, 'The last time I crossed here, five weeks ago, something happened which revolutionized the whole of my life. We had George Mueller of Bristol on board. I had been on the bridge twenty-four hours and never left it. George Mueller came to me and said, 'Captain, I have come to tell you that I must be in Quebec Saturday afternoon.' 'It is impossible,' I said. 'Very well, if your ship cannot take me, God will find some other way. I have never broken an engagement for fifty-seven years. Let us go down into the chart-room and pray.'

I looked at that man, and thought to myself, what lunatic asylum can that man have come from?

I never heard of such a thing as this. 'Mr. Mueller,' I said, 'do you know how dense the fog is?' 'No,' he replied, "my eye is not on the density of the fog, but on the Living God, Who controls every circumstance in my life.'

He knelt down and prayed one of the most simple prayers, and when he had finished, I was going to pray; but he put his hand on my shoulder, and told me *not* to pray. 'First, you do not believe He will answer; and second, I BELIEVE HE HAS, and there is no need whatever for you to pray about it.'

I looked at him and he said, 'Captain, I have known my Lord for fifty-seven years, and there has never been a single day that I have failed to get an audience with the King. Get up, Captain, and open the door, and you will find the fog gone.' I got up, and the fog was indeed gone. On Saturday afternoon, George Mueller was in Quebec for his engagement."

This story amazes me every time I read it in my devotional. I covet the simple faith some have and George Mueller is an inspiration to me as I hope he is to everyone.

I believe if our trust and faith were but more simple, we should just take Him at His word; and our lives would be all sunshine in the sweetness with our Lord. Don't let any 'fog' stand in your way today from receiving from God. Pray. There is never a time when we fail to get an audience with the King!

Write how you see the difficulties in your life and the faith you have in Jesus.

Day 22 – It's Personal

Trying to be a good Christian, I once wanted to share my faith with a girl who said she just didn't 'buy into' Christianity. I went on and on about how God drew my heart to Him, the times God answered prayer, all the miracles in my life, *and* I also mentioned how God talks to me.

It is impossible for me to talk about God in my life without mentioning this little fact too.

Well, this set off a chain of events that I ended up finding a little funny, but not really funny. The events have stifled me just a little. Apparently, this young lady told a man who was our superior about God 'talking to me,' who then wrote an email to our medical director (boss), who then got together with the other 'boss' who then they both asked me to lunch. When we were having lunch, the two lady bosses very sincerely and politely asked if I was 'ok' and if they could do anything for me.

Needless to say, I was a little confused. As we continued to talk, they asked if I was mentally stable - in so many words - and if I needed any mental help. As I tried to decipher what they were trying to get at, I asked if they were asking if I was mentally ill? They did not directly answer; and I affirmatively stated I was *not* mentally ill - not that I am aware of anyway. (ha ha) I have a nursing background and know that 'hearing voices' is one of the cardinal signs of schizophrenia - a serious mental illness - and is not something one can hide or not be aware of having - or at least others around the affected person are aware.

We ended our time together on a good note, however, it was later that I connected the dots and figured what happened. I think the young girl heard my testimony - that God talks to me - and told the superior man, who felt that was 'crazy' talk, and he then proceeded up the chain of authority.

In any event, the Bible tells us - '...and they overcame him (the devil) by the blood of the Lamb, and by the word of their testimony...' I believe our testimony has great and profound effect on others and in the spirit realm. I think it is personal to everyone how God came into their lives and has power because it is truth and it is a testimony of the great grace and power of the living God to change hearts and lives. I believe this is the greatest thing we can do is to simply and honestly share with someone what God has done for us.

I want to continue to share my testimony to everyone who will listen and, yes, I still share how the God all Creation talks to me! I love when He talks to me and it is the most important thing that happens to me in life and I know that I know that I know His voice. Jesus said, 'My sheep hear My voice, and I know them, and they follow Me.'

One friend asked how she could have God talk to her. I was not sure, but I told her to just ask Him and He always answers our prayers. John 10.27. One friend always said, "God's always talking and He's always working" and I agree with that.

Write how God talks to you and your testimony.

_____
_____
_____
_____
_____
_____
_____
_____
_____
_____
_____
_____
_____
_____
_____
_____
_____
_____

Day 23 – Faithful

We had been hearing about Hurricane Dorian in 2019 for what seemed like weeks. I prayed for the Bahamas who experienced her full force a few days before. It broke my heart to hear a young mother ask for prayer for her and her baby because her baby is only four months old.

We weathered Dorian very well. She passed us and moved up the coast to other locations. We prayed for all who were in potential danger. God is faithful. There was a time a few days before I felt frightened. I was told there was a mandatory evacuation ordered for me in the area I live in. I have never had to leave because of a storm before. The good news is that she went from a category 5 hurricane to a 'cat 2' - what we affectionately call our Florida storms.

As I am thankful for being spared in this storm, I praise my God for His faithfulness to me and my elderly father who lived with me and my animals. I know he was frightened too. We are ready to go home if it is the time for God to call us, but we are happy to stay here as well.

God is faithful. But we always need to pray. I believe it altered the course of the storm.

I sing along with the Hymn - "Great is Thy Faithfulness, Morning by morning new mercies I see. All I have needed, His hand has provided, Great is Thy Faithfulness, Lord unto me."

The Bible encourages me to have faith in God because He is truly faithful. There are times that faith is very difficult, but the Bible also tells me that my lack of faith does not stop the faithfulness of God and any chance of my prayers being answered. 2 Timothy 2.13 assures me - "..if we are faithless, He remains faithful [true to His word and His righteous character], for He cannot deny Himself." I am grateful because sometimes I am weak.

I also pray the Word, "When my strength fails, do not forsake me" (Psalms 71.9) It amazes me how complete the Word of God is, He does know everything - everything we face, everything we feel, everything we fear, everything that makes us settled, just plain everything.

We have been very blessed and are going to take a deep breath and hope for the best. We believe God will get us through anything.

Write how you feel about the faithfulness of God.
_____
_____

Day 24 –Holy

My brother and I loved visiting rivers like this one. He would ask, "When's your next day off?" He made plans for us to have a great day. Sometimes it seemed like we did the same thing each day, but one of the many things I loved about my brother is how each time we did the same thing, he loved it and seemed to be so excited - like it was the very first time we were doing that thing.

He would tell me about the river the entire ride to the location. He would put the boats in and be excited to push me off into the river. As we traveled down the river, he always remarked how serene and beautiful it was. He really loved the time spent with nature on a river or doing whatever else we had decided to do that day.

I think God wants us to come with the joy that is ours about knowing Him and coming to Him in prayer and spending time in His Word - like it is all brand-new to us. Sometimes that is not as easy as I wish. I get tired sometimes and when I read His Word, I sometimes say, "yes, I have read that section a million times it seems,' and I sometimes gloss over the parts I am familiar with. Not happy that I do that. I have been in prayer for a spirit that cherishes every word in the Word of God no matter how many times I have read about John the Baptist baptizing Jesus. I pray for the awe I felt the first time I ever read the words that touched my heart deeply and every word.

The Word of God challenges me to always remember to not treat the holy things of God as if they are not holy, but common or mundane. Leviticus 22.32-33 tells me, "You must not treat Me as common and ordinary. Revere Me and hallow Me, for I, the Lord, made you holy to Myself and rescued you from Egypt to be My own people! I am Jehovah!"

"...beware that you do not treat the holy gifts ... as though they were common..." Numbers 18.32.

I pray daily to reverence God and the things of God each and every day and remember God is Holy and has called me to revere Him. I want to treat Communion, His Word, Prayer, Worship, Church, sharing my faith and all the things of God with excitement and joy. I want to tell the Lord He is 'new every morning' like His love and mercy for me. (Lamentations 3.22-23)

Write your ways of how you keep God's things holy and fresh in your life.

_____
_____
_____
_____

Day 25 –Abundance

    While talking to a friend one day about the abundance and faithfulness of God, she said, "Yeah, I prayed for a coat and received FIVE." She did not pray for five, but God is good. I chuckled as I remembered once I prayed for shoes and then it seemed I had more than I could count. I shared my over-abundance of shoes with others I knew did not have any. Yes, I think God is a God of abundant supply and we cannot out give God, so I give and God gives. "The Lord is our Shepherd; we will not lack." Psalm 23.1

    At church one day, the piano played a song I loved the first time I ever heard it - it is the hymn "He Giveth More Grace"

He giveth more grace when the burdens grow greater,
He sendeth more strength when the labors increase;
To added affliction He addeth His mercy,
To multiplied trials, His multiplied peace.

When we have exhausted our store of endurance,
When our strength has failed ere the day is half done;
When we reach the end of our hoarded resources,
Our Father's full giving is only begun.

His love has no limit, His grace has no measure,
His pow'r has no boundary known unto men;
For out of His infinite riches in Jesus,
He giveth, and giveth, and giveth again.

Romans 8.32 reminds me -"He who did not withhold *or* spare [even] His own Son but gave Him up for us all, will He not also with Him freely *and* graciously give us all [other] things?"

I have lived the Words "... to Him Who, by (in consequence of) the [action of His] power that is at work within us, is able to [carry out His purpose and] do superabundantly, far over *and* above all that we [dare] ask or think [infinitely beyond our highest prayers, desires, thoughts, hopes, or dreams]—To Him be glory in the church and in Christ Jesus throughout all generations forever and ever. Amen (so be it)." Ephesians 3.20-21.

My brother had nothing. He was released from prison with a felony record, no job, no money, ill health, and more. My pastor and I prayed. God opened up a flood gate and my brother received a check for over $60,000.00 with which he purchased his first and only brand-new vehicle that he cherished and enjoyed for many years. He received a sizable monthly income that allowed him to have shelter, food, and doing all the things he loved to do while he lived out his last nine years here. God gave us superabundantly above all I ever asked or thought possible. Praise Him for everything.

From a personal perspective, I was not wise and did not have a retirement. Sometimes I was ashamed to ask God in the face of choices I had made. He is faithful and true to His Word. I am facing retirement soon and He has provided over $300,000.00 for me at this late time in life. I ask myself, "How much does one need?" I have always had my daily bread; but am grateful to the God Who can do anything and does everything.

The Word challenges us, "Bring all the tithes (the whole tenth of your income) into the storehouse, that there may be food in My house, and prove Me now by it, says the Lord of hosts, if I will not open the windows of heaven for you and pour you out a blessing, that there shall not be room enough to receive it."

God truly does give and give and give again. No fear of exhausting Him. All He wants in return is little old us.

Write how God meets your needs and how you present your tithes to him.

_____
_____
_____
_____
_____
_____

Day 26 – What Others Remember

Elephants are one of my favorite animals. I think they are beautiful and amazing creatures. I understand 'elephants never forget.' Exactly what *do* they never forget? Apparently, they never forget most things in their up-to 60-year lifespan. Their memory is their key to survival.

Elephants' superb memories help them stay alive in ways that go beyond just recognizing threats. Females that come from desert climates can remember where reliable water can be found and are able to guide their herds to water over very long distances; even over the span of many years. This is a pretty clear indication that elephants have a great ability to remember details about their spatial environment for a very long time.

They also remember each other. I read a story recently of an elephant named Jenny that became very animated when a new elephant named Shirley arrived. After the caretakers looked into the animals' backgrounds, they discovered the two had performed with the same circus for only a few months—22 years earlier. Amazing.

Recently, I have been reminded of two incidents where family members have 'remembered' something I did or did not do many, many years ago. One was about my reasons for running away as a young girl and the other about when I was asked for help and did not. I have few regrets in life, however, being reminded of incidents I have no personal memory of makes me wonder what else others remember that I may have forgotten. I wondered how many times these memories came to my family members and how often they were saddened by them. I am saddened to know they held these memories in their hearts for so many years. For all I know, there may be more.

Sometimes I try to edit the things I find disappointing in life - apparently especially my disappointments to others. I choose to remember the good times and the good things I have experienced, but I know others may remember an event I have long forgotten; an event I wish I could have done differently or said I was sorry for. I may have been a troubled younger person and made mistakes; but am hoping I am a better older person and making less mistakes.

The Bible tells me God remembers things. He remembers His covenant with His children, His promises to care for us, that we are weak, all the times we tried so hard, all the times we did do the right things, when prayers need answered, He remembers how He loves us, everything about us - even the number of hairs on our heads and what makes us happy and more.

God encourages us to remember things too - how He saved us each time we asked, the miracles He did for us, His Word and promises, His sacrifice, His love, His commandments, the poor and others, our past and bondage, how hard families worked to make it and give us life, the ones who loved and cared for us and still do, and more.

God, however, does not remember everything. He never remembers our forgiven sin, our mistakes, our bad days, or when we were disappointing. And for this I am grateful. I want to forget the wrongs done to me too and hope those that I have wronged can forgive me and remember the better things.

Write how you have chosen to forgive others and pray they have forgiven you as well.

Day 27 – Good Friday

Good Friday comes each year. Sometimes it seems like just yesterday we had ashes placed on our foreheads for the start of the Lenten season. And, it always happens that we come to the time to remember what our Savior did for us so many years ago and all this means today.

Before each Good Friday, many, many years ago, Jesus had supper with His followers. He told them what was going to happen, promised everything would be alright, and then He went to the Garden of Gethsemane with a few disciples. "....And being in an agony He prayed more earnestly: and His sweat was as it were great drops of blood falling down to the ground." Luke 22.44. How many nights I have agonized over my life situations or my loved ones? I always thought God did not understand the agony of the human condition, however, I was wrong, He is well acquainted with agony as well as sorrow and grief and sin even though He never sinned or deserved punishment.

I once heard a story that asked, "What is the very strong emotion to a person who is very difficult and terrible to us or has done very wrong things?" Most answered 'hate,' and at first that is what I would think I would answer. But the truth is there is another answer. An answer that took time to sink in - it is Jesus' answer. He answers, 'Love.' Love is His response to those who hate Him, those who praised Him just a week before and now want Him dead, those who falsely accused Him, those who spit on Him, those who dragged Him to be humiliated in front of kings and jeering crowds demanding He be killed even though He healed many among them and fed them and was kind to them and did no wrong. Jesus responds in love to the ones who shoved a crown made of painful thorns on His head and beat His back, stripped Him and mocked Him and those who put Him on a Cross and drove nails in His hands and feet. He answers to forgive them and continues going to the Cross where He suffers an unimaginable death to save us and love us.

For 'no one has greater love [no one has shown stronger affection] than to lay down (give up) his own life for his friends.' John 15.13. And '...but God shows *and* clearly proves His [own] love for us by the fact that while we were still sinners, Christ (the Messiah, the Anointed One) died for us. Romans 5.8.

God's reaction to my sin, disobedience, stubbornness, pride, lack of faith, disinterest, hate in my heart against others who wronged me, and more is not hatred and disgust with me, but mercy and love and forgiveness. I am thankful as I remember the Lamb of God Who came to live and die for me and the whole world. The Lamb of God Who takes away the sins of the world. John 1.29.

Write how you remember what Jesus did every Good Friday and every Easter morning.

Day 28 – Do This in Remembrance

It's easy to forget. Sometimes it's great to forget. Great to forget difficult moments in life, accidents that were devastating, job loss, hurtful words, times we thought we'd never make it through, and more. Sometimes we forget so we can remember only the good things in life.

On the other hand, memories are precious. It's great to remember. Great to remember good friends, good times, achievements, fun parties, past vacations, and more. Many of us have pictures or mementos that remind us of special moments or special people in our lives.

It seems to me that God knows how easy it is to forget and tragically how easy it is to forget Him and how much He did for us so many years ago. In His Word, He reminds us to continually remember God. All the goodness in my life is from the Hand of the Father. I want to remember each day how He came into my life to give me His life and His truth, and His deliverance and love. I want to remember His care for me and what He did to care for me.

Luke 22.19-20 tells us – "Then He took a loaf [of bread], and when He had given thanks, He broke [it] and gave it to them saying, 'This is My body which is given for you; do this in remembrance of Me.' And in like manner, He took the cup after supper, saying, 'This cup is the new testament *or* covenant [ratified] in My blood, which is shed (poured out) for you.'"

So, what did He do for us? Isaiah 53.4-10 tells us -"Surely He has borne our griefs (sicknesses, weaknesses, and distresses) and carried our sorrows *and* pains [of punishment], yet we [ignorantly] considered Him stricken, smitten, and afflicted by God [as if with leprosy]. But He was wounded for our transgressions, He was bruised for our guilt *and* iniquities; the chastisement [needful to obtain] peace *and* well-being for us was upon Him, and with the stripes [that wounded] Him we are healed *and* made whole. All we like sheep have gone astray, we have turned everyone to his own way; and the Lord has made to light upon Him the guilt *and* iniquity of us all. He was oppressed, [yet when] He was afflicted, He was submissive *and* opened not His mouth; like a lamb that is led to the slaughter, and as a sheep before her shearers is dumb, so He opened not His mouth. By oppression and judgment, He was taken away; and as for His generation, who among them considered that He was cut off out of the land of the living [stricken to His death] for the transgression of (all) people, to whom the stroke was due? And they assigned Him a grave with the wicked, and with a rich man in His death, although He had done no violence, neither was any deceit in His mouth. Yet it was the will of the Lord to bruise Him; He has put Him to grief *and* made Him sick. When (God) make(s) His life an offering for sin [and He has risen from the dead, in time to come], He shall see His [spiritual] offspring, He shall prolong His days, and the will *and* pleasure of the Lord shall prosper in His hand."

He gave His life to give me mine. Praise be to God. I pray to always be in remembrance of Him.

Write what keeps you in remembrance of the things of God

_____
_____
_____
_____
_____
_____
_____
_____
_____
_____
_____
_____
_____
_____
_____
_____
_____
_____
_____
_____

Day 29 – New Year 2019

Every New Year's Eve around the world, people sing the Scottish song Auld Lang Syne. Most do not know the words, they just muddle along (like me), some know the Scottish version, and a few know the English translation. I included the two versions below.

Traditional Song	Modern English Translation
Auld Lang Syne Should auld acquaintance be forgot, And never brought to mind? Should auld acquaintance be forgot, And days o' langsyne! **Chorus:** For auld langsyne, my dear For auld langsyne, We'll tak a cup o' kindness yet For auld langsyne!	**Times Gone By** Should old acquaintances be forgotten, And never brought to mind? Should old acquaintances be forgotten, And days of long ago! **Chorus:** For times gone by, my dear For times gone by, We will take a cup of kindness yet For times gone by.

We twahae run about the braes, And pu'd the gowans fine, But we've wander'dmony a weary foot Sin' auld langsyne. We twahaepaidl't in the burn Frae morning sun till dine, But seas between us braid haeroar'd Sin' auld langsyne. And there's a hand, my trusty fiere, And gie's a hand o' thine, And we'll tak a right guid willie-waught For auld lang syne! And surely ye'll be your pint' stoup, And surely I'll be mine! And we'll tak a cup o' kindness yet For auld langsyne!	We two have run about the hillsides And pulled the daisies fine, But we have wandered many a weary foot For times gone by. We two have paddled (waded) in the stream From noon until dinner time, But seas between us broad have roared Since times gone by. And there is a hand, my trusty friend, And give us a hand of yours, And we will take a goodwill drink (of ale) For times gone by! And surely you will pay for your pint, And surely I will pay for mine! And we will take a cup of kindness yet For times gone by!

Auld langsyne - what does it mean? I never really knew until recently. It's about friends and remembering things past and present. New Years is about the future too and making friends and having things to remember again.

We all walk through the years together. Some are glad when one is behind and looking forward to better ahead. I wish and pray for that for everyone too. Looking back, there are things I wish I had the opportunity to do over again, but we all know that is not possible. I do not want to live with regret; however, I pray to learn from mistakes I made, friends I hurt or disappointed, things I should have done differently, and my list is quite long sometimes. I wish I had spent more time in prayer and trusting God more. I wish I had helped friends more and been kinder. Wish I made better work decisions and more. I will make New Year's resolutions to do these things and pray I can do better as I walk into all our New Years.

I take a cup of kindness for memories of old, but "I press on toward the goal to win the [heavenly] prize of the upward call of God in Christ Jesus." Philippians 3.14. I cannot change the past, but I hope I can change the future.

Write how you will see God in each New Year and how you remember friends.

_____
_____
_____
_____
_____
_____
_____
_____
_____
_____
_____
_____

Day 30 –Freedom

Happy 4th of July each year! This day we celebrate our Independence and Freedom from a tyrannical government to embark on a new nation! With the help of God and men of prayer, we established a land for the free and a home for the brave.

It has been a very long time since I have heard this song, but I love the **Battle Hymn of the Republic.**

"Mine eyes have seen the glory of the coming of the Lord
He is trampling out the vintage where the grapes of wrath are stored
He hath loosed the fateful lightning of His terrible swift sword
His truth is marching on.....

In the beauty of the lilies Christ was born across the sea
With a glory in His bosom that transfigures you and me
As He died to make men holy, let us die to make

men free
While God is marching on

Glory, Glory, hallelujah!
Glory, glory, hallelujah!
Glory, glory, hallelujah!
His truth is marching on"

Yes! God wants all men to be free. Not only free in their daily lives, but in their spirit as well. He died to make men holy and well and free and forgiven and more. "...The Lord sets free the prisoners..." Psalm 146.7

2 Peter 1:2 tell me, "May grace (God's favor) and peace (which is perfect well-being, all necessary good, all spiritual prosperity, and freedom from fears and agitating passions and moral conflicts) be multiplied to you in [the full, personal, precise, and correct] knowledge of God and of Jesus our Lord."

I recently heard someone who struggles with addition pretty much say, "It's never beatable - it's always a problem; even when you do not engage in your addiction." I believe God can do anything. I believe He can break any chain that has us bound. I believe He is able to heal the deepest pain and help anyone overcome the most heart and mind wrenching situations. He wants everyone free.

".....Blessed (celebrated with praises) is the King Who comes in the name of the Lord! Peace in heaven [freedom there from all the distresses that are experienced as the result of sin] and glory (majesty and splendor) in the highest [heaven]!" Luke 19:38

My bondage had its roots in deep seated anger. When I asked God to show me the reasons for my bondage to depression and anxiety and defeat, He showed me; not to condemn me, but to set me free - "So if the Son liberates you [makes you free men], then you are really and unquestionably free." John 8:36

Galatians 3:13 reminds me "Christ purchased our freedom [redeeming us] from the curse (doom) of the Law [and its condemnation] by [Himself] becoming a curse for us." Free of worry, free of addition, free of sorrow, free of whatever drags you down and causes anxiety or fear.

He paid too high a price to have my soul just stirred at times, but never really changed - or set free like He died to do.

Write about what you want more of.

_____
_____
_____
_____
_____
_____
_____
_____
_____
_____
_____

Day 31 – Lent

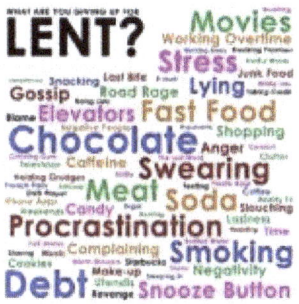

After each Ash Wednesday, we enter into the 'Lenten season.' It is the Christian season that is a period of 40 days before Easter. It is a time many Christians choose to fast, repent, do things in moderation, practice self-denial of certain enjoyable activities, or work on spiritual discipline in areas they feel could use some improvement. To many, the purpose of Lent is to take time for reflection on Jesus Christ—His suffering and His sacrifice, His life, death, burial, and resurrection.

Before He was crucified, Jesus spent time with His disciples. He prepared them. He told them about the soon-to-be events. He told them how He would be taken, beaten, and crucified. He told them they would abandon Him, but it would be alright afterward. He told them one of them would be the one to betray Him. He knew Peter would deny Him three times. Jesus knew everything and He spent the time before He left them preparing them and telling them how He knows everything; and everything has a plan and purpose.

Jesus could have called thousands of angels to rescue Him, but then He would not have been able to rescue us. His sacrifice and choosing to surrender have been the very thing that saves us all today from every failure, every mistake, and every regret. His sacrifice has allowed us to be healed and well. His sacrifice allows us to become the children of God.

During the six weeks of each Lenten season, I commit to self-examination and reflection. Some Christians who observe Lent may make a commitment to fast, or give up something—a habit, such as smoking, watching TV, or a food or drink, such as sweets, chocolate, or coffee. I want to make a commitment to read my Bible and spend more time in prayer to draw nearer to God. Some strict observers may not eat meat on Fridays, often opting for fish instead. The goal of my spiritual choices is to strengthen my faith and develop an even closer relationship with God.

I admit my sacrificial intentions usually only last about 6 or 7 days when I try to do things to become a better person and better Christian. I would be happy to give up stress and procrastinating and many of my other 'bad' habits. Truth be told, I have been a miserable failure at trying to do better in many areas. I don't want to just give up complaining, fearing, bad attitudes, lack of concern for others, and all my other shortcomings for 40 days, but forever.

I thank Jesus for choosing to come to Earth, be born a Baby, live His life, and suffer and die on a Cross to be raised from the dead three days later for me. I realize I do not have to suffer because He already has, but I want to reflect on Him and His goodness this season and all to come.

Share how you celebrate the season of Lent.

_____
_____
_____
_____
_____
_____
_____
_____
_____
_____
_____
_____
_____
_____
_____
_____
_____
_____
_____
_____
_____
_____
_____
_____
_____
_____
_____

Bonus Day – Perfect

Got a call from an old friend.... Sad news. Cancer. We cried. We talked about all the times we spent together - all the talks, all the laughs, all the cries, all the sharing our day, all our hopes and fears, all our everything. Our friendship. The thing we treasure most in life.

She talked about hoping to go to heaven. I said, "Do you want to go to heaven?" She said, "Yes!" I said, "All you have to do is tell Jesus you want to go to heaven! It's that simple." We cried. She talked about going even though she does not want to and waiting for me to come in (hopefully) years to come. We cried again. I told her how much I will miss her and how I want to talk every day we can and not cry; but laugh and remember and tell each other how much our friendship has meant to each of us. We do not know how long it will be.

I know I should be dancing. Another child of God gets to go home. Gets to walk the streets of gold. No more tears, no more sadness, no more money trouble, no more watching others we love suffer and be lost, no more bad news headlines, no pain, no more medical reports, just Paradise. Home with Jesus, finally. Strangely enough, I cry.

Another girlfriend and I talked about our other losses and we agree - heaven is PERFECT. Who wouldn't want to be home? There, everything and everyone is perfect. Sometimes I wish it was my time to go home so even I, too, can be perfect. Imagine that, I thought I already was and am perfect. Turns out, I need to be home before I am perfect. When I get home I will always say the right thing, think the right thing, be polite, have patience, love the way I wish I could always do now, never be afraid again, understand all the things that do not make sense to me here, see the ones I lost and miss, and cast my crown at the feet of my Savior, Jesus. I will be home and perfect.

The sun is setting for some today. I say, 'wait for me Grandpa and Grandma and Aunts and Uncles and Brothers and Mom and Dad and many others I have loved that are home now - I will be there soon. Too soon.'

Are you missing someone? Has someone been told tough news? How will you help them in this season of life?

_____
_____
_____
_____
_____
_____

Bonus Day – He left the grave behind Him

A little boy born with Down syndrome attended his third-grade Sunday School class faithfully each week. As you can expect, the other children did not readily accept the boy because he seemed different.

The Sunday after Easter, their teacher brought in small boxes--one for each child. The children were told to go outside, find some symbols of new life, and put them in their containers. So, the children ran wildly throughout the property looking for something to fill their boxes.

Once they returned to the classroom, they began to share their discoveries with the class. One by one they opened their boxes to show flowers, butterflies, leaves, and more. Each time the class would "ooh" and "ahh."

Then the child with Down syndrome opened his box to reveal nothing inside. The children exclaimed, "That's stupid! It's not fair! He didn't do the assignment right!"

The little boy exclaimed, "I did so do it! It's empty...because the tomb where Jesus laid was found empty!"

Jesus left the grave behind Him. What does that mean for us? If Jesus had not risen from the dead, our faith would be foolish and fake. But He did rise from death, confirming His life and message. The resurrection of Jesus is the basis for our hope of life eternal beyond the grave and for everything we need in Him each and every day. Because He is alive, we also live in eternity and here.

After Jesus rose, His promise in John 14.16 - '...and I will pray the Father, and He shall give you another Comforter, that He may abide with you forever..' was fulfilled.

Not only is the Spirit of God our Comforter, He is our Teacher to teach us everything and the One to bring all things to our remembrance - all things Jesus has to say to us. John 14.26.

Also, just like the first followers, we are blessed with power. "But ye shall receive power, after that the Holy Ghost is come upon you: and ye shall be witnesses unto me ... unto the uttermost parts of the earth." Acts 1.8

And, just like the disciples we can be filled with His Spirit - "And when they were come in, they went up into an upper room ... (the disciples) all continued with one accord in prayer and supplication, with the women, and Mary the mother of Jesus, and with His brethren." Acts 1.13-14 "And when the day of Pentecost was fully come, they were all with one accord in one place. And suddenly there came a sound from heaven as of a rushing mighty wind, and it filled all the house where they were sitting. And there appeared unto them cloven tongues like as of fire, and it sat upon each of them. And they were all filled with the Holy Ghost, and began to speak with other tongues, as the Spirit gave them utterance. Acts 2.1-4

God's triumph over death is our triumph and He planned for us to be given His Spirit to continue with His power and love to do the work He designed us to and be delivered as we need to be. Praise the Lord for His Unspeakable Gift. 2 Corinthians 9.15

Amen.

Write your thoughts about how the empty grave is meaningful in your life.

_____
_____
_____
_____
_____
_____
_____
_____
_____
_____

www.ingramcontent.com/pod-product-compliance
Lightning Source LLC
Chambersburg PA
CBHW041129110526
44592CB00020B/2738